the 100
BEST
BRAIN
TEASERS
FOR KIDS

Interior and Cover Designer: Richard Tapp
Art Producer: Sara Feinstein
Editor: Erin Nelson
Production Editor: Nora Milman

Illustration © 2021 Moko Ko
Author photo courtesy of Natasha Vermilyea

ISBN: Print 978-1-64876-803-3 | eBook 978-1-64876-229-1
R0

the 100 BEST BRAIN TEASERS FOR KIDS

A MIND-BLOWING CHALLENGE OF WORDPLAY, MATH, AND LOGIC PUZZLES

DANIELLE HALL

ILLUSTRATIONS BY MOKO KO

ROCKRIDGE PRESS

CONTENTS

HI! I'M ACE . . .

I am a wizard from the planet Witloo. My pronouns are they/them. It's so nice to meet you. I know you're just the Earthling to help me solve these 100 brain teasers.

On Witloo, the Beloved Crystal keeps our planet in balance. Prankster wizards from the planet Flarkspur have taken the Beloved Crystal and hidden it somewhere here on Earth. Without the Beloved Crystal, my planet would face endless rainy days. That may not seem like such a bad thing, but most Witloomites are afraid of water! I don't think the Flarkspurians know that, though. They're really just a bunch of pranksters.

Will you help me find the location of the Beloved Crystal? It's hidden under five levels of protection challenges. Each level includes logic puzzles, math problems, and wordplay that are all designed to stump you. There are also a few riddles and head-scratching jokes. The levels will get more difficult as you go on. Since most of these puzzles come from the history and cultures here on Earth, your knowledge is the key. Working together, I just know we can find the Beloved Crystal and bring peace to our world.

Do you see that cat? That's Panther, my trusty sidekick. He will roam the pages and hunt for clues to help you solve the brain teasers. If you get stuck on a puzzle, you can find Panther's clues on page 72. Panther has at least one clue for every puzzle. You can face the challenges in any order, so if you're perplexed, just move on to another puzzle and come back later.

Let's get started! The Crystal awaits!

10 TEASER TIPS

Hi! I'm Panther, and I'll help you find clues to the Flarkspurians' puzzles. Cats are very smart and curious (if I do say so myself), and Witloomite cats are the smartest around. This isn't the first time the Flarkspurians have left us with difficult puzzles to solve. Here are 10 things I've learned about their puzzles. I think these tips will help you as you get started!

1. **Think:** Do you know what the puzzle is asking you to do? Read the puzzle twice before you start to solve it to make sure you understand it.

2. **Restate:** Put the puzzle in your own words. This can help make the puzzle simpler. Oftentimes, Flarkspurians include extra information to distract you. Putting a puzzle in your own words can help you identify the unnecessary elements.

3. **Consider:** Have you solved a simpler version of the puzzle before? Like Ace said, you come from a species of riddle-makers and problem-solvers. If you've solved a version of a puzzle before, how did you do it? Use this knowledge as a starting place.

4. **Draw:** Jotting down a grid can help you figure out an answer. Many logic problems can be solved more quickly if you set up a chart to help you remove the incorrect answers.

5. **Experiment:** Sometimes you'll need to use trial and error to solve a puzzle. For example, if you are asked to find a number between 1 and 10 that meets certain characteristics, try testing a middle number. Do you need a higher or lower number? Trial and error will help you move forward.

6. **Be careful:** If you're solving a riddle, you'll want to look out for special riddle tricks. One common trick that Flarkspurians rely on is to use words with double meanings. For example, a riddle might ask you to name a thing that *roars*. This would probably make you think of a lion, but the answer could be a fire—which *roars* if it's very loud.

7. **Pause:** If you get frustrated by a puzzle, it's okay to take a break. This is a good rule in life, too, by the way—it's okay to step away from a challenge and take a few deep breaths.

8. **Ask for help:** It's not cheating to use my hints in the Clues section on page 72 for help with a puzzle. Don't worry! I don't like spoilers. I'm an expert at giving you just enough help without ruining the puzzle.

9. **Reread:** Once you think you have the answer, read back through the puzzle and check to make sure your answer works.

10. **Above all, have fun!**

6. **Be careful:** If you're solving a riddle, you'll want to look out for special riddle tricks. One common trick that Flarkspurians rely on is to use words with double meanings. For example, a riddle might ask you to name a thing that *roars*. This would probably make you think of a lion, but the answer could be a fire—which *roars* if it's very loud.

7. **Pause:** If you get frustrated by a puzzle, it's okay to take a break. This is a good rule in life, too, by the way—it's okay to step away from a challenge and take a few deep breaths.

8. **Ask for help:** It's not cheating to use my hints in the Clues section on page 72 for help with a puzzle. Don't worry! I don't like spoilers. I'm an expert at giving you just enough help without ruining the puzzle.

9. **Reread:** Once you think you have the answer, read back through the puzzle and check to make sure your answer works.

10. **Above all, have fun!**

Level 1

SMARTY-PANTS

Let's get started on some brain teasers! Don't forget you can ask for Panther's help by going to the Clues section on page 72. The Flarkspurians are tricky but fair—they'll start by going easy on you. So put on your thinking cap and dig right into the first puzzle!

1 AMAZING ANAGRAMS

An anagram is a word made from the rearranged letters of another word. For example, the words **HORSE** and **SHORE** are anagrams of each other. Try to find the anagram below.

The first word is something you do while your friend tells you a story or your teacher is teaching. The second word describes an old kind of movie where there was no sound. The answer has six letters.

2 DITLOIDS: CALENDAR AND TIME

A ditloid is not some sort of creature from the planet Witloo. It is a little puzzle that combines wordplay and math. Ditloids are common sayings or objects that have been turned into numbers and initials. The Flarkspurians think this puzzle will stump you, but I know you can figure it out! Here is an example: **60 M in an H** is "60 minutes in an hour." Can you discover the meanings of the ditloids below? They all have to do with the calendar and time.

7 D in a W

28 D in F

10 Y in a D

3 SHELLEY'S JOURNEY

MATH

Shelley the tortoise is at the bottom of a 10-foot-tall hill. She can climb 4 feet per minute, but she can only climb for 1 minute before taking a break. She needs to rest for 30 seconds before starting again. Each time she stops, she slides back down 2½ feet. How long will it take Shelley to climb the hill?

4 PUZZLING PALINDROME

WORDPLAY

A palindrome is a word or number that is the same forward and backward. LEVEL is an example of a palindrome.

What is a one-word palindrome that describes a vehicle that goes very fast?

5 COMPOUND CONUNDRUM

WORDPLAY

A compound word is made of two smaller words. For example, a "ballgown" is a gown worn to fancy parties known as "balls." A "birthday" is the day of one's birth.
Find this compound word:

The first word is a hen's baby. The second word is something that comes from a pod and might be part of your dinner. Together, they are a food often used in Middle Eastern cooking.

RIDDLE A: Why couldn't the chicken hit a home run?

6 FIND THE LIAR

You've arrived in a Flarkspurian city where two groups of people live. One group has only truth-tellers and one group has only liars. In this city, you meet Bip and Bop. Bip and Bop may both belong to the truth-telling group, may both belong to the lying group, or may be in different groups. Based on the statement below, is Bip a liar or a truth-teller?

Bip says, "We are both liars."

Panther says, "Bip cannot be a truth-teller, because then they would tell you they were a truth-teller. If you need more clues, just let me know and I'll help you out. You can always turn to page 72 to seek help."

FUN FACT: This type of logic puzzle is known as a "Knights and Knaves" puzzle or a "Liars" puzzle. It was first made popular by mathematician Raymond Smullyan. You'll see other examples in this book. These puzzles are common in pop culture and have appeared in movies like *Labyrinth* and television shows like *Doctor Who*.

7 WORD LINKS

Find the word that makes each set of words into two new words or expressions. In each puzzle, the first new word will be created with the first word and the missing middle word. The second new word will be created with the missing middle word and the last word. Good luck!

Here is an example:

RAIN_____ _____TIE

Answer: BOW

(RAINBOW and BOWTIE)

Try these:

TOOTH _____TALE

FIRE _____BALL

MASKING _____ MEASURE

8 WHAT NUMBER AM I?

LOGIC

I am a four-digit number whose digits add up to 10.
   None of my digits are 0 and none of my digits repeat.
   My first number is the greatest and I am even.
   My first two numbers and my last two numbers have the same sum.

9 A TERRIFYING SCENARIO

MATH

Camila was walking on the boardwalk with 15 members of her dance team. When it started to rain, all but 3 of them squeezed into the Taffy Shop. How many were left in the rain? (Remember, we Witloomites are afraid of water. Help!)

10 MIXED-UP BAKING

LOGIC

Jasmine just finished baking to celebrate Eid, and she's trying to remember the order she baked everything. She baked almond cookies, yogurt cake, and meskouta (an orange cake). Jasmine baked the almond cookies right before the yogurt cake. The meskouta wasn't last. In what order did Jasmine bake everything?

RIDDLE B: What is the smartest kind of worm?

FLARKSPURIAN TRICK STICKS: THREE SQUARES

Remove three Trick Sticks from the puzzle below so only three squares remain.

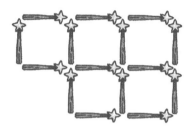

 RIDDLE C: Imagine you're on a space station in a locked room. The doors are all sealed, and the only window looks out into space. You have no materials to break out and no way to call for help. How do you get out?

12 A REMARKABLE REBUS

In a rebus puzzle, you "read" the puzzle to figure out the expression that's being illustrated. You often have to take the puzzle literally. This is definitely an Earthling expression, so I'm counting on you!

Example:

———
READ
———

Answer: Read between the lines.

Please help me figure out the rebus below:

SECRET
SECRET

13 MYSTIFYING MATH

The Flarkspurians have left you a math riddle to solve. Hmm . . . perplexing!

I am a prime number between 1 and 20. Multiply me by 9 and divide me by 3. Then subtract 3 from the answer and you'll have 30. What am I?

14 BLANKOUT

In this puzzle, the Flarkspurians have removed all the vowels from this quote. Fill in the blanks with vowels to complete the quotation from those tricksters!

"R_ _D TH_S _ _T L_ _D:
FL_RKSP_R_ _NS _R_ SM_RT_R TH_N
W_TL_ _M_T_S. H_H_!"

RIDDLE D: What do a picnic, playing cards, and pool all have in common?

WORD LADDER: CHANGING SEAN INTO WILL

A word ladder is a type of puzzle that challenges you to transform one word into another in a series of steps. You can only change one letter for each step. The positions of all the other letters stay the same. Each step will create a new English word. The Flarkspurians have been nice enough to give you a clue for each step.

SEAN

___ ___ ___ ___ **Close an envelope**

___ ___ ___ ___ **Get money for an item**

___ ___ ___ ___ **The bottom part of a window**

WILL

ODD WORD OUT

In this type of puzzle, all but one of the objects have something in common. Can you find the object that is different from the rest?

spinach

lemonade

broccoli

mango

peas

RIDDLE E: What five-letter word becomes tinier when you add two letters to it?

WORD LADDER: CHANGING A MULE INTO A GOAT

Here's another word ladder, like the one you saw on page 8. Change one letter per step and keep all the other letters in the same positions. Each step must be an English word. This one is a bit trickier—the Flarkspurians have left off one of their ladder clues!

M U L E

__ __ __ __ **A rodent that digs**

__ __ __ __

__ __ __ __ **Water around a castle**

G O A T

TANGLED RELATIONS

This type of puzzle is known as a relations puzzle, and it has to do with the connections between different family members. Try figuring this one out. Remember that Panther is around to help if you need a clue!

If the only brother of your father's only sister only has one child, what is that child's relationship to you?

TRICKY CHANGE

Here's a math puzzle from the Flarkspurians that has to do with American Earthling coins. Since Witloomites are not familiar with Earthling money, can you figure it out?

Yeison has six coins that can be pennies or dimes or a mix of each. What are the possible total amounts of money he has?

TRIANG 123

One, three, and six are triangular numbers. Do you see how you can use them to visualize a triangle? Find the other triangular numbers up to 36.

CRYSTAL CHALLENGE #1

You did it! You completed the first level of puzzles. Great job!
    What's this? It's a message for us from the Flarkspurians.
It looks like another puzzle with some symbols below it. Oh!
I know this trick. The Flarkspurians have written the answer
in code. If you figure out the answer to the riddle, you'll
know what letter each of those symbols stands for. I bet this
will help us find the Beloved Crystal! Keep track of which
letters go with each symbol on page 66. That will make future
challenges easier!

Ancient, I am running.
I loom above them all—
Ever down and never up,
With roaring as my call.

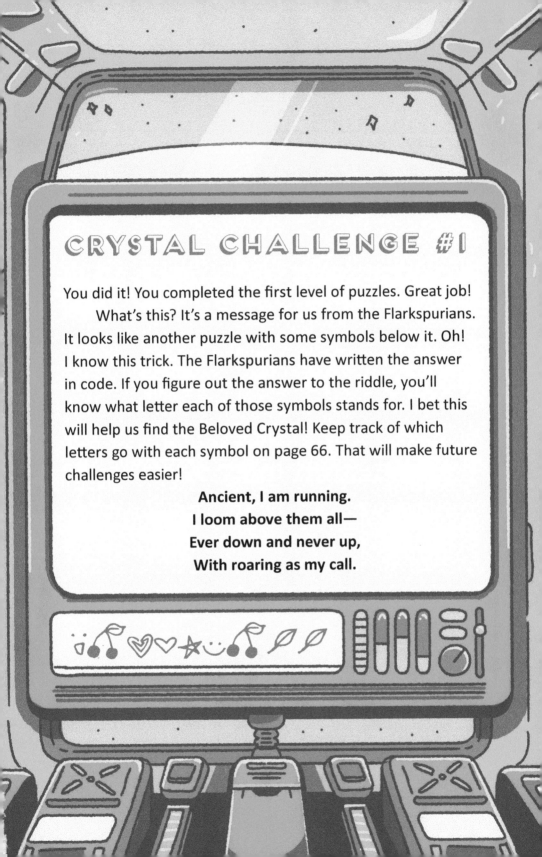

CRYSTAL CHALLENGE #1

You did it! You completed the first level of puzzles. Great job!
    What's this? It's a message for us from the Flarkspurians.
It looks like another puzzle with some symbols below it. Oh!
I know this trick. The Flarkspurians have written the answer
in code. If you figure out the answer to the riddle, you'll
know what letter each of those symbols stands for. I bet this
will help us find the Beloved Crystal! Keep track of which
letters go with each symbol on page 66. That will make future
challenges easier!

Ancient, I am running.
I loom above them all—
Ever down and never up,
With roaring as my call.

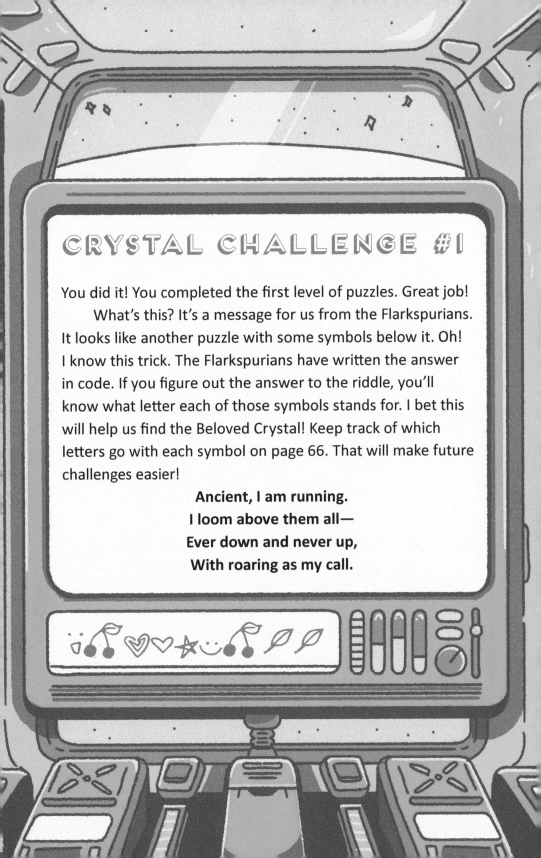

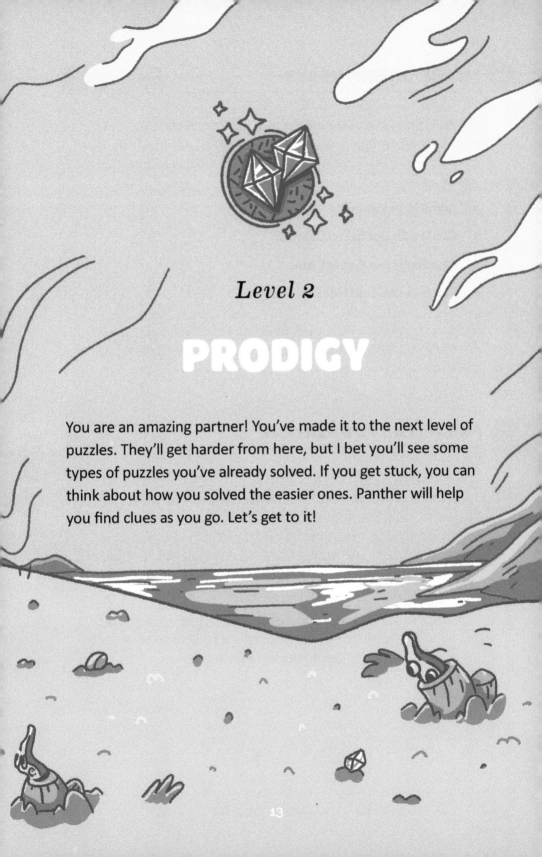

Level 2

PRODIGY

You are an amazing partner! You've made it to the next level of puzzles. They'll get harder from here, but I bet you'll see some types of puzzles you've already solved. If you get stuck, you can think about how you solved the easier ones. Panther will help you find clues as you go. Let's get to it!

MIXED-UP BIRTHDAYS

LOGIC

Jayna, Olivia, and Azeema are all different ages (8, 9, and 10 years old) and have different birth months (March, August, and October). Find each person's age and birth month using the clues below.

1. **Jayna is 10 years old.**

2. **Olivia was not born in March.**

3. **Azeema is not 8 years old.**

4. **Azeema was born in October.**

This is so fascinating! Your solar years here on Earth are only 365 days, but on Witloo, a year is 1,171 days. I'm only 3 Witloomite years old.

22 FUN WITH SPOONERISMS

WORDPLAY

A spoonerism is any saying with mixed-up words that still makes sense. Wonder why this teaser has a funny name? Reverend William Archibald Spooner was famous for mixing up his words! For example, he once said, "The Lord is a shoving leopard," instead of "The Lord is a loving shepherd." Now these mix-ups are used for humor and wordplay. See if you can figure out what object this clue is describing.

This is something you could use to get around the neighborhood, or, according to Spooner, a "well-boiled icicle."

23 AMAZING ANAGRAMS

WORDPLAY

You're looking for two words that contain the same five letters. The first word is what it takes to start a fire. The second word names green places in a city.

24 PUZZLING PALINDROME

WORDPLAY

Find a one-word palindrome that is the name of a gym exercise. To do one of these is an accomplishment; to do many is epic!

25 WHAT'S THE PROBLEM?

MATH

Input the numbers 1 through 6 to make the formula correct. You'll use each new number only once. Panther is standing by if you need a little hint to get your answer!

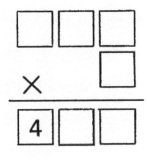

RIDDLE F: What's the difference between a haunted Canadian forest and a barnyard with a lot of geese but only one duck?

26 DITLOIDS: ENTERTAINMENT LOGIC

Given only initials and numbers, can you discover the hidden meanings of the ditloids below? They all have to do with stories for kids.

101 D

S W and the 7 D

3 L P

27 SHELLEY'S STILL CLIMBING! MATH

Since we last saw Shelley the tortoise, she's gotten faster. She's at the base of the same 10-foot-tall hill. Now she can climb 5 feet per minute. She still has to take a break every minute and rest for 30 seconds. When she rests, she still slides back down 2½ feet. How many minutes does it take her to climb the hill now? My, my! Earth has such strange creatures. Look at the shell on that one!

28 AMAZING ANAGRAMS WORDPLAY

Find a pair of words that contain the same letters. The first word is the part of the body that contains the funny bone. The second word is often used to describe something underneath something else.

29 FIND THE LIAR LOGIC

Skootle and Skeetle come from a Witloomite city where one group of residents always lies and one group always tells the truth. Identify whether each is lying or telling the truth.

Skootle says, "We are both from the same group."
Skeetle says, "We are both from different groups."

30 TANGLED RELATIONS LOGIC

Look! Another Earthling relations puzzle. The Flarkspurians have always been curious about Earthling families!

Your father only has one sibling. What relation would your father's sister's sister-in-law be to you?

 RIDDLE G: How can one person become two?

Can you read the following quote? It sort of looks like Earthling writing!

ᴎɘmɒɘɿb ɒ ʜɟiw ꙅniǫɘd mɒɘɿb ɟɒɘɿǫ yɿɘvƎ

ᴎɒmduT ɟɘiɿɿɒH-

FUN FACT: Mirror writing is a simple type of "code" that has been used by artistic and literary geniuses like Lewis Carroll and Leonardo da Vinci. This isn't really a code, but it can confuse someone enough to safeguard a message. These messages are written backward and can be held up to a mirror to be "decoded." It may feel funny at first to write this way, but you can improve with practice! Try it for yourself.

Kamu holds a key to a Flarkspurian spaceship. It looks like clear plastic with a design on it:

He flips the card once horizontally, once vertically, and then turns it 90 degrees clockwise. Which of the following choices matches what Kamu sees now?

A REMARKABLE REBUS

Oh, another fun rebus puzzle! Can you figure out what this one says? The first step is to read the puzzle literally and see if it makes you think of anything ...

m ce

m ce

m ce

COMPOUND CONUNDRUM

Find a compound word where the first part describes a dog's ears in the wind and the second part is a boy from a nursery rhyme who climbs a hill. Together, they form a nickname for a popular breakfast food.

 RIDDLE H: What did the clock do when it was hungry?

MYSTIFYING MATH

Can you write an equation that comes to a total of 1,000 using eight 8s? The numbers in the equation can include more than one 8 each, as long as there is a total of exactly eight 8 digits in the equation when you are finished. For example, you could do $88 \times 888 + 8 - 88$ (this is not the right answer).

TRICKY TRIPLETS

This type of puzzle asks the reader what three seemingly unrelated objects have in common. Here is an example: Swiss cheese, bowling ball, donut. Answer: They all have holes.

Now you try! What do a map, a padlock, and a laptop all have in common?

 RIDDLE I: What is the creature that walks on four legs in the morning, two legs at noon, and three legs in the evening?

HOW MANY SQUARES?

The Flarkspurians want to know how many squares you can find in the shape below. Remember, a square has four equal sides. Count carefully! The Beloved Crystal depends on it!

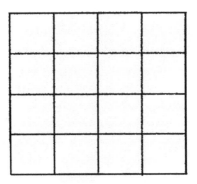

WORD LADDER: CHANGING A BULL INTO A BEAR

At each step of this word ladder, change only one letter from the word before. All the other letters stay in the same positions. Each step must be an English word. Good luck!

BULL

— — — —

_ _ _ _ **A thing that buckles**

— — — —

BEAR

FLARKSPURIAN TRICK STICKS: SIX SQUARES

Move only two Trick Sticks to create six squares.

 RIDDLE J: The more you take from me, the bigger I become. What am I?

WORD IN HIDING

In this type of puzzle, the Flarkspurians hide a word in plain sight. The phrase contains both the word and the key to solving it. For example: Early in the year, **A**shley, **p**lease **r**ide **i**nto **L**ansing. "Early" tells you where to find the letters in the answer. "In the year" hints that you're looking for something related to time or the calendar. The answer is "April."

Find the word hidden in the phrase below. The answer has four letters.

Before all else, Noona is considerate ever.

CRYSTAL CHALLENGE #2

Wow! You're doing great! You completed all the Prodigy level challenges. The Flarkspurians sent me another message. They don't think you'll be able to solve this puzzle, but I believe in you! You're so creative and clever. I know Witloo is in good hands.

All the words below have something in common, except one. Find the odd word out.

pot

jar

rat

dog

ton

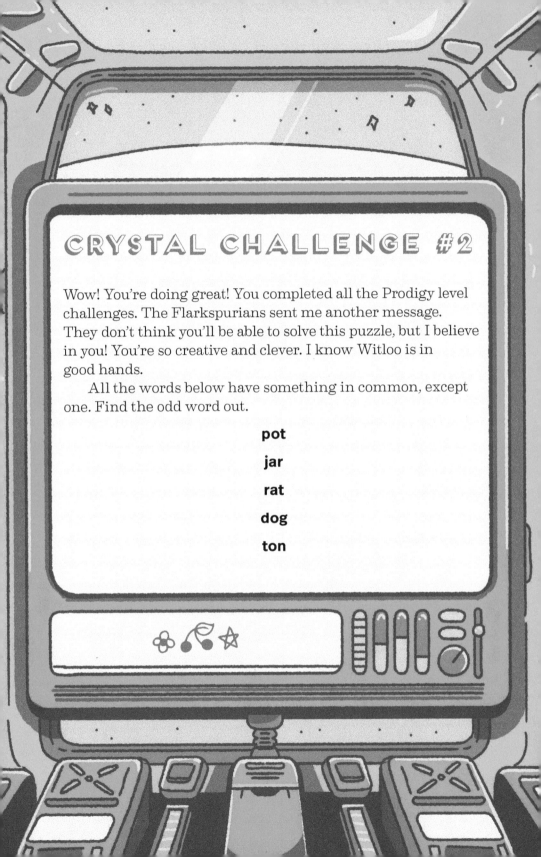

Level 3

BRAINIAC

Phew, that was tough! This next level will be a little bit harder—but you're nearly halfway through 100 puzzles. Remember, you can always take a break if you get stuck or tired. It takes a lot of brainpower to save a whole planet! And remember, if you need help, Panther will be on the lookout for clues. You can find these on page 72.

WHICH HOUSE?

Arjun, Sheyln, Mariam, and Staci live on the same street. Their houses are red, green, blue, and gray, but not necessarily in that order.

1. **Sheyln and Staci live across the street from the green house.**

2. **Arjun's house is blue.**

3. **Staci lives next door to the red house.**

Who lives in the gray house?

42 TRICKY CHANGE

MATH

Dylan has 20 coins. One-half of the coins are quarters. One-fifth of the coins are nickels. One-fourth of the coins are dimes. He also has one penny.

What is the value of the change in Dylan's pocket?

43 AMAZING ANAGRAMS

WORDPLAY

Here's another anagram for you to try! The first word is someone who follows someone else—maybe in a game of tag. The second word is the act of looking for something.

44 ALPHAMETIC

MATH

Each number in the following number sentence has been replaced with a letter. Find the numbers to make it correct.

GO + GO = WOO

Wow! Do you Earthlings greet each other by saying, "Go, go, woo!"? Hah, just kidding. Panther assures me this is a math puzzle that just looks funny.

RIDDLE K: What's the difference between a gardener and a clothes basket?

PAINTING PROJECT

You and your friends have 15 wooden cubes and some black and gold paint. How many different ways can you paint the cubes if you paint each face a solid color? A cube has six sides by definition, and you won't need all 15 cubes. Panther says, "Two cubes are the same pattern if they can be flipped or turned to look exactly like each other. So, for example, if you paint one face gold, it doesn't matter which one it is."

 RIDDLE L: On what day of the week are most twins born?

46 FIND THE LIAR

LOGIC

These liar puzzles are so tricky! I guess that's why another word for a prankster is a "trickster," huh? These Flarkspurians sure are clever.

One of TyQuaisa's five classmates took her pencil case. Four of them are lying about what happened. Interestingly, the thief is telling the truth. Can you identify who took the pencil case?

Harley says, "Simone is the thief."

Lauren says, "Yes, Simone is the thief."

Jaquan says, "Simone is definitely the thief."

Ingrid says, "Lauren lied."

Simone says, "Lauren told the truth."

47 WORD LADDER: CHANGING LEAD INTO GOLD

WORDPLAY

At each step of this word ladder, change only one letter from the word before. Change one letter per step and keep all the other letters in the same positions. Each step must be an English word.

LEAD

— — — —

— — — —

GOLD

Brainiac   29

Once upon a time, a farmer went to a market and purchased a wolf, a goat, and a cabbage. On his way home, the farmer came to the bank of a river and rented a boat. Unfortunately, the boat could only carry the farmer and only one of his purchases: the wolf, the goat, or the cabbage.

If left unattended together, the wolf would eat the goat, and the goat would eat the cabbage.

The farmer's challenge was to carry himself and his purchases to the far bank of the river, and have all of his purchases at the end. How did he do it?

Oooof! This puzzle is so tricky! You may need to write some stuff down to figure it out. I'm glad you're helping us. Flarkspurian puzzles really make my head spin.

RIDDLE M: Dancing on the wind, a bird without wings. Free except for a string. What am I?

49 MARBLE MANIA

There's a bag of 21 marbles on the table in front of you. Inside, 7 marbles are black, 7 are blue, and 7 are purple. Without looking inside the bag, how many marbles would you have to pull out to be guaranteed at least one matched pair?

50 COMPOUND CONUNDRUM

Find a compound word where the first part describes how you might feel on a summer day and the second part describes a faithful furry friend. Put the words together and you get a BBQ specialty.

51 DITLOIDS: FUN AND GAMES

You are getting really good at ditloids. I can't wait for you to figure these out! All of these ditloids have to do with Earthling games and gadgets.

3 S and you're O

2 W on a B

52 C and 2 J in a D of C

A cryptogram is a puzzle that uses substitution. In the following code, each letter of the alphabet has been substituted for another. All the words use the same code and follow the same theme. Can you figure out all the words for these kids' animated movies by breaking the code? Panther says, "I figured out that X is A! Anywhere you see an X, you can write an A above it."

1. **SKXZX (2016)**

2. **HXUJ (2006)**

3. **MTQ LURZHQJJ XZE MTQ CUKF (2009)**

4. **AQXBMW XZE MTQ AQXJM (1991)**

5. **TKO MK MUXRZ WKBU EUXFKZ (2010)**

6. **CRZERZF ZQSK (2003)**

7. **TKSQ (2015)**

8. **UQE JTKQJ XZE MTQ JQPQZ EOXUCJ (2019)**

FUN FACT: One type of puzzle with real-world uses is codemaking and codebreaking. This is known as cryptology. Throughout history, military leaders have encoded messages to send to spies and soldiers. Now we also use codes to keep our data secure. Are you interested in historical codebreakers? Look up Virginia Aderholt, who led one of the US Army's language units in World War II. She was the first to intercept a message of surrender from the Japanese! Her feats in codebreaking saved many lives.

53 JACINTA'S PET PROBLEM

Jacinta has a lot of pets! She is sending old pet toys to some other pet lovers. She can fit 8 large pet toys in a shipping box or 10 small ones. She has a total of 96 toys. If she has more large pet toys than small toys to send, what is the least number of boxes she needs?

54 THREE IS COMPANY

What do pumpkins, turkeys, and your initials all have in common?

55 WORD IN HIDING

Find the word hidden in the phrase below. Remember, like the puzzle you saw on page 22, one of these words will tell you *where* to find the letters for the word and one of them will give you a hint about *what* you're looking for. The answer has four letters. Panther is standing by if you need help. He knows these can be difficult.

Lastly, animals delighted to wag tails.

An algorithm is a series of instructions to complete a task. The algorithm below leads to a treasure. Use the algorithm to find the treasure. Then color the square where the treasure is located.

Code: Move forward one square : → Move backward one square: ← Move up one square: ↑ Move down one square: ↓ Color in the square with the treasure: 🔵

START		

Instructions:

1. →
2. →
3. ↑
4. ↑
5. 🔵

FUN FACT: Today, we write codes for computers to get them to carry out complex operations. In the 1800s, Ada Lovelace (1815–1852) was an English mathematician and writer who became one of the first computer programmers. She worked with Charles Babbage on an early machine known as the Analytical Engine and published the first algorithm for that machine.

WORDS IN HIDING

The Flarkspurians love hiding things in plain sight! Can you find the animal in each phrase? The animal names could be split over two or three words to hide them. Here is an example: Lucas wants to **be a r**adio host. (bear) Now try to solve these!

1. **For real, I only want to play video games.**

2. **Don't panic! A melting chocolate bar still tastes good.**

3. **Talaya kicked the ball and scored a goal.**

4. **Can tea terrify you? Just ask Reuven.**

RIDDLE N: I sit in a corner and travel around the world. What am I?

WORD LADDER: CHANGING CATS INTO MICE

At each step of this word ladder, change only one letter from the word before. Keep all the other letters in the same positions. Each step must be an English word. It looks like the Flarkspurians haven't left any hints this time! They really are stepping up the difficulty.

C A T S

— — — —

— — — —

— — — —

M I C E

59 CHANGE-A-LETTER

Find a word for the person who officiates a baseball game. Change one letter of that word to find the name of a large area under the control of one ruler.

RIDDLE O: Which playing card has the biggest heart?

60 PAPER FOLDING

If you take a sheet of paper and fold it in half, fold it again, fold it again, fold it again, and then fold it in half again, how many sections would you have?

CRYSTAL CHALLENGE #3

Wow, you did an amazing job with the Brainiac puzzles! Here's the next Crystal Challenge puzzle from the Flarkspurians. Can you figure out this riddle? Surely, it'll get us one step closer to the location of the Beloved Crystal.

Travel somewhere over me to reach Oz.
Rest assured when you see me after the storm.
I am a phenomenon of water and light,
My colors move to cool from warm.

Level 4

MASTERMIND

I'm so lucky to have your help! Thanks for trying so hard to help Witloo. Let's see what the Flarkspurians have in store for you in the Mastermind level.

WHO WANTS ICE CREAM?

Four friends, Gaspard, Yuma, Mahé, and Anna, went out for ice cream. They each ordered a different flavor and a different topping. Using only the clues below, figure out who got which flavor and topping. We don't have ice cream on Witloo, but if we did, I think I'd be a chocolate fan!

1. **Gaspard didn't get vanilla ice cream, but did get cherries on top.**

2. **Mahé doesn't like peanuts or fudge sauce.**

3. **The person who got peanuts also got mint ice cream.**

4. **Anna got chocolate ice cream.**

Here is a chart to help you figure it out!

	GASPARD	MAHÉ	YUMA	ANNA	CHERRIES	PEANUTS	FUDGE	CARAMEL
VANILLA								
CHOCOLATE								
STRAWBERRY								
MINT								
CHERRIES								
PEANUTS								
FUDGE								
CARAMEL								

CHANGE-A-LETTER

Find a word meaning "something you plan to do." Change one letter to make a word that describes a brilliant new contraption.

RIDDLE P: Which day does an egg hate the most?

FINISH THE FORMULA

Fill in the number sentence below with the numbers 1, 2, 3, and 4. Each number will be used only once and the answer will be 14. Play around until you get the right answer!

$$(\underline{\quad}/\underline{\quad}) + (\underline{\quad} \times \underline{\quad}) = 14$$

In a quotefall, you'll drop the letters from the top columns into the grid below. Keep each letter in the same column. Each letter will be used once. When you drop them all correctly, you'll reveal a quote from Jason Reynolds, the author of *Long Way Down, Ghost,* and other young adult books.

FIND THE LIAR

There are three people—Kofi, Sara, and Maritza. One of them is a knight, one a knave, and one a spy. The knight always tells the truth, the knave always lies, and the spy can either lie or tell the truth.

Kofi says, "Maritza is a knave."
Sara says, "Kofi is a knight."
Maritza says, "I am the spy."

Who is the knight, who is the knave, and who is the spy?

PUNNY ANSWERS

Even Flarkspurians have a sense of humor! The following question has a fun pun in the answer. By the way, Iceman is a superhero, but that doesn't really matter for the clue. Can you figure out the answer?

What is Iceman's favorite band?

FUN FACT: This puzzle is based on a real crossword clue that read: "Iceman's favorite band." Alex Briñas developed the clue, which appeared in *The New York Times* crossword in 2017 as a "debut word." This means it had never been used in that crossword puzzle before! For crossword constructors like Alex, having a certain number of "debut words" is an awesome achievement.

Input the numbers 2, 3, 4, and 9 to complete the long division problem.

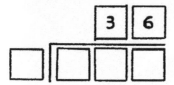

You may be unfamiliar with long division! Here, I made it a multiplication problem for you. Remember, the numbers 2, 3, 4, and 9 each appear one time in the remaining boxes.

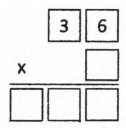

FLARKSPURIAN TRICK STICKS: SEVEN SQUARES

LOGIC

Look at the Trick Sticks below. Can you move only two Trick Sticks to create seven squares? You may not break sticks or overlap them.

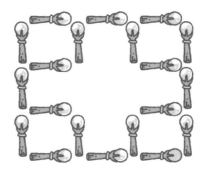

RIDDLE Q: I'm tall when I'm young and short when I'm old. What am I?

Write an algorithm, or a series of instructions, to help Ace get to the Beloved Crystal. Ace can't go through fire (OUCH!) or move diagonally. Use the code on page 34 or make up your own. This is good practice for when we really need to find the crystal!

Code: Move forward one square : → Move backward one square: ← Move up one square: ↑ Move down one square: ↓

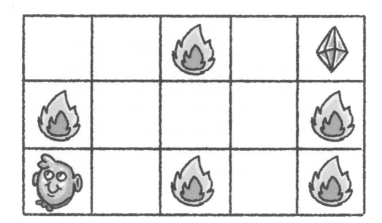

70 TANGLED RELATIONS

Another relations puzzle! Some Earthlings have very complicated families! Read the statement carefully to figure out the relationship.

Tim tells Cooper, "Your mother's mother's daughter is my sister in-law." What possible relationship(s) could Tim have to Cooper?

RIDDLE R: We sit on a bridge and stare out, guarding our charge inside. Everyone who sees us sees themselves, and wonders what we hide. What are we?

71 DITLOIDS: GROOVY GROUPS

Can you figure out the hidden meanings of the ditloids below? They all have to do with groups of things.

26 L of the A

12 S of the Z

7 W of the W

Here's a cryptogram puzzle that is hiding Earthling book titles. Each of the book titles below uses the same code. Can you break the code and figure them all out?

1. **XZPNV CHNSGTL HLK UQZ FRYQULRLY UQRZB**

2. **H DPRLSFZ RL URWZ**

3. **H FTLY DHFS UT DHUZP**

4. **WHURFKH**

5. **ZF KZHBT**

6. **YQTGUG**

7. **TJU TB WV WRLK**

8. **QJPPRNHLZ NQRFK**

FUN FACT: In World War II, the Allies needed a new code the Axis powers couldn't understand. The Navajo code talkers saved the day! These soldiers saved countless lives with secret codes developed from their own tribal languages! For each letter, the code talkers used a Navajo word for an animal. That word would represent the first letter of its English translation. For example, if they wanted to transmit the letter C, they would say *moasi*, meaning "cat." In 2000, President Bill Clinton awarded the code talkers the Congressional Gold Medal.

WORD LADDER: CHANGING HEAD INTO TAIL

At each step of this word ladder, change only one letter from the word before. The positions of the other letters stay the same. Each step will create a new English word. You must be a master at these by now. Panther is standing by, just in case!

HEAD

— — — —

— — — —

— — — —

— — — —

TAIL

MARBLE MANIA

You have three bags of marbles: one containing only white marbles, one with only black marbles, and one with black and white marbles mixed together. Each bag is labeled incorrectly. That means that none of their labels match the actual contents. What is the fewest number of marbles you need to draw to be certain of the contents of each bag? (And no peeking!) Panther says, "Don't lose your marbles over this one. Take your time and think it through! You'll get it!"

WORD LADDER: CHANGING WEAK INTO FIRM

At each step of this word ladder, change only one letter from the word before. Change one letter per step and keep all the other letters in the same positions. Each step must be an English word. Panther says, "The fifth word in this list (the one in the very middle) is the word for a group of cattle."

W E A K

— — — —

— — — —

— — — —

— — — —

— — — —

— — — —

— — — —

F I R M

RIDDLE S: Long teeth of white and black, voices chomping with each smack, and yet even as my mouth is full, I am oh so musical!

76 TANGLED RELATIONS

Can you figure out who is looking at the photo? A man is looking at a photograph. When you ask him who it is, the man says "Brothers and sisters, I have none. That man's father is my father's son."

77 SEEING THREE

What do marigolds, mustard, and canaries all have in common?

78 WEB SUM

I'm so glad you're here, Earthling! The Flarkspurians know that Witloomites are much better with words than numbers. Here's another puzzling math problem for you. Enter the numbers 1 through 9 one time each into the web below so that each line (vertical, horizontal, and diagonal) adds up to 15.

HOLIDAY HAUL   LOGIC

You and four friends all got some money for the winter holidays. You want to figure out the average amount of money that everyone got, but keep everyone's amount secret. You have a calculator. How can you solve this problem? Panther says, "You'll enter a number into the calculator before you pass it."

 RIDDLE T: I have 6 faces, but no mouth. I have 21 eyes, but cannot see. I bring gain or loss to those who throw me. What am I?

A REMARKABLE REBUS   WORDPLAY

You've had some practice with rebus puzzles. Check this one out. What do you think it is trying to say?

7s8a2f4e9ty3

CRYSTAL CHALLENGE #4

You've done an amazing job of the Mastermind level. The other Witloomites will sing songs about your heroics! Here's the next Crystal Challenge from the Flarkspurians. Be sure to look at those symbols carefully—we are close to finding the Beloved Crystal. I'm sure of it!

Answer each clue below to find the secret letter. Unscramble the letters when you finish to reveal a secret word.

____ 1. Find an expression you might say when something is gross. Change one letter to describe what you could do to a T-shirt. The new letter is your secret letter.

____ 2. Change a letter in HOPE to get a tool. The new letter is your secret letter.

____ 3. Find a word for a rabbit's jump. Double the vowel. Now change one letter to describe a type of circle. That is your secret letter.

____ 4. Examine FOREVER and subtract a homophone for a number. Add a sometimes-vowel to the remaining word. The letter you add is your secret letter.

____ 5. Add a letter to ONE to get a shape. This is your secret letter.

____ 6. Find a four-letter word meaning "by yourself." Add another letter without changing the meaning.

____ 7. Begin with a heavy amount. Add a letter to make a sound. Add one more letter to make a natural object. This is your secret letter.

In case you need a reminder, a homophone is when words sound the same, but are spelled differently. *There* and *their* are homophones!

Level 5

GENIUS

Four levels down, one level to go! Hang in there, friend. You don't mind if I call you *friend,* right? You're certainly acting like one: loyal and hardworking in order to save us Witloomites. Thank you so much! Let's get working, Genius. We are almost there, but these puzzles will really test your thinking skills.

This classic riddle is an adaptation of the Alcuin's River Crossing problem you saw on page 30. Four people want to cross a river at night. The only way across is a narrow bridge, and the only source of light is a single torch. Each time a person crosses, they must use the torch. The bridge can only hold two people at a time. Someone must return the torch to the starting side to give it to the next person.

Person A is the fastest and can cross the bridge in 2 minutes. Person B takes 4 minutes. Person C takes 10 minutes. Person D is the slowest and takes 16 minutes to cross the bridge. If the torch only lasts 30 minutes, what steps can they take to make sure everyone gets across safely?

82 NUMBER SEQUENCE MATH

Find the next number in this tricky sequence.

3, 7, 15, 31, 63, . . .

83 QUIRKY CONNECTIONS LOGIC

What do Jupiter, Alaska, and an ostrich have in common?

 RIDDLE U: Remember Spooner (page 14)? Here's a riddle he'd enjoy: What's the difference between an orca in a tuxedo and a story of throwing everything away?

84 AMAZING ANAGRAMS WORDPLAY

Find the name of people who study space. Then jumble the letters from that word to create a funny phrase. This phrase describes what happens when part of what those people study disappears.

Panther says, "The Flarkspurians spend a lot of time looking through telescopes and studying space. That's how they know so much about Earth! Do you know what a person who studies the night sky is called?"

85 WEIGH DAY FOR JACINTA'S PETS

MATH

Jacinta has several dogs, cats, and tortoises. She picks three pets at random and weighs them. The first pet is twice as heavy as the second pet. The second pet is three times as heavy as the third pet. How much does each pet weigh if altogether their weight is 20 pounds?

86 ODD WORD OUT

LOGIC

Four of these words have something in common, but one of them is the odd word out! Which one is it?

produce, record, marker, object, rebel

87 ALPHAMETIC

MATH

Each letter in the problem below stands for a number. What are those numbers?

LMNO

× 4
_____

ONML

COMPOUND CONUNDRUM

WORDPLAY

Find a compound word where the first part is an old form of transportation you might find on a ranch. The second part is a root vegetable that's sometimes red and white. Put together, they make a spicy condiment.

 RIDDLE V: I lose my head in the morning, but I get it back at night. What am I?

89 **DYNAMIC PREPOSITIONS**

WORDPLAY

You're looking for one word that can create two expressions with different meanings. For example, even though "throw" is used in "throw away" and "throw up," the meanings are very different!

Would you help me find the answer to this puzzle?

If you pair the word with "up," it means to delay something. The word paired with "on" is a grip for dear life. What's the word?

Place eight queens on an 8 × 8 chessboard so that none of them can attack each other. Queens can move any number of squares diagonally, vertically, or horizontally.

FUN FACT: This puzzle was originally created by Max Bezzel in 1848. There are interesting versions for other chess pieces as well, like kings, rooks, and knights. Chess players, mathematicians, and computer programmers love chess puzzles, so there are many types of these games available.

91 FLARKSPURIAN TRICK STICKS: AN EQUATION!

LOGIC

Make this number sentence true by adding three Trick Sticks.

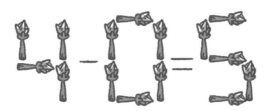

92 A REMARKABLE REBUS

WORDPLAY

Can you find the saying illustrated here? Remember, a rebus puzzle is a visual representation of an expression. Panther says, "Mmm, sounds delicious!"

4 3.1_159

93 IMPOSSIBLE POSITIONS

LOGIC

Hina is standing behind Maddie and Maddie is standing behind Hina. How is this possible?

RIDDLE W: To be used, it must be thrown away. When you no longer need it, you pull it back to you. What is it?

MYSTIFYING MATH

Using numbers 1 through 6 exactly once each, find the largest possible product of two numbers with three digits. For example, one possible answer is 123 × 456 = 56,088. However, this isn't correct. What is?

RIDDLE X: What flows like water, even though it's completely dry?

ALPHAMETIC

Each number in the following equation has been replaced with a letter. In this alphametic, with a touch of humor, M is not zero. Can you figure out what number each letter stands for?

SEND

+ MORE

MONEY

WORD IN HIDING

Find the five-letter word hidden in the phrase below. The phrase contains both the word and the key to solving it, so read carefully. Before you start, Panther says, "unpredictably" must mean the letters could be anywhere in the words.

Unpredictably, a fruit growing clustered at happy vineyards.

 97 **JACINTA'S CAT CONUNDRUM**

MATH

Jacinta has three cats. Mr. Mittens is three times Peppa's age. Irving is twice as old as Peppa. Added together, their ages total 30 years. How old is each cat?

RIDDLE Y: How can someone go eight days without sleep?

98 **PYRAMID OF PENNIES**

MATH

You have 10 pennies arranged like the grid below. By moving just three pennies, you can turn the pyramid upside down. Panther says, "You'll have one penny at the top and four at the bottom."

99 DYNAMIC PREPOSITIONS

WORDPLAY

You did so well on the last puzzle like this that the Flarkspurians want to try to stump you with a new one. They don't know who they are dealing with! Can you find the word?

If you pair the word with "on," it's what a friend might say if they're running just a couple minutes late, but want to go with you. Paired with "out," it could be what you're doing when you meet a friend for ice cream.

RIDDLE Z: I help you time travel—turning back the clock—meeting old friends and laughing at old jokes. I am created in mere seconds, but I last forever. What am I?

100 THE WALKING STICK CHALLENGE

LOGIC

Keshun visited his grandfather in the country for his birthday. As a gift, his grandfather made him a walking stick that was 5 feet long. However, Keshun had to take the bus back home, and the bus doesn't allow any items longer or taller than 4 feet. He didn't want to leave the gift behind. How did he solve this conundrum? Panther says, "He doesn't have to bend, break, cut, or change the walking stick."

CRYSTAL CHALLENGE #5

The Flarkspurians are very impressed that you've made it this far! They really didn't think anyone from the planet Witloo could find an Earthling as smart and persevering as you. This is the last Crystal Challenge, and I'm sure it'll tell us where the Beloved Crystal is hidden . . . unless, of course, the Flarkspurians have another trick up their sleeves.

The names of 25 American states are hidden in the columns below, but each state's name is missing a letter. Enter the letters A through Z in the shaded boxes below to reveal the names. Each letter is used only once. These letters are not necessarily in order, and Q is not used. When you're finished, find the hidden state in the middle row. Panther says, "You can complete this in any order, so go for the easy ones first."

1	2	3	4	5	6	7	8	9	10	11	12	13	14	15	16	17	18	19	20	21	22	23	24	25
A	M	I	M	A	O	M	T	R	A	I	N	N	O	C	F	M	F	B	L	B	N	R	G	V
V	A	D	A	N	C	I	E	H	R	N	I	A	R	O	L	A	R	T	O	I	E	H	E	I
E	R	E	R	N	A	C	N	O	I	G	A	N	C	L	O	S	H	O	U	R	W	M	O	R
R	K	H	Y	B	L	A	N	D	N	E	M	K	A	O	R	S	O	H	I	M	H	I	I	W
M	T	I	N	O	A	R	S	M	E	O	N	E	L	I	I	A	D	I	S	I	A	S	O	I
O	E	O	E	R	O	I	O	I	W	R	E	N	I	L	N	A	E	I	I	C	M	S	W	S
T	A	A	A	G	L	O	T	S	E	I	R	U	O	I	H	K	S	A	L	I	S	A	O	O
N	S	S	D	O	A	N	A	O	R	A	A	C	R	N	I	A	L	H	A	G	H	I	M	N
E	A	H	A	N	H	A	H	U	S	O	S	K	N	O	O	N	A	O	S	A	I	N	I	S
V	N	I	L	T	O	L	C	R	E	W	K	Y	I	I	D	S	N	N	K	N	R	E	N	I
R	S	N	E	R	M	A	A	I	Y	A	A	A	A	S	O	A	D	E	A	C	E	B	G	N
T	A	T	W	I	A	S	R	S	A	N	L	S	P	N	L	S	E	W	N	H	O	R	A	G

THE FINAL CRYSTAL CHALLENGE

Okay, now we have five words from the Crystal Challenges, but they don't make any sense . . . what now? Wait . . . I'm getting a message from the Flarkspurians . . . This new puzzle has some familiar symbols in it. I bet the words that you already figured out for the previous five Crystal Challenges are part of this message. Put them in first. They will help you figure out the letters for the rest of the symbols. Use the chart below to record your discoveries. Beloved Crystal, we are almost there!

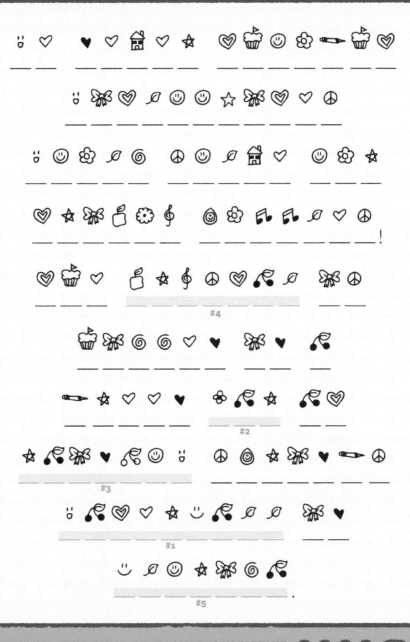

#4

#2

#3

#1

#5

You did it! You figured it out.
Hold on tight. and I'll teleport us to that location. Thank you
so much for finding our Beloved Crystal! You truly are a
hero and friend to all of Witloo. I'll be sure to call on you if
the Flarkspurians ever play a prank like this again. In the
meantime. farewell. fantastic friend!

RIDDLE ANSWERS

A. She kept hitting FOWL balls!

B. A BOOKworm

C. Stop imagining!

D. They can all use a table (picnic table, card table, pool table).

E. Short or small

F. One has ghostly moose and one is mostly goose.

G. By using a mirror

H. It went back four seconds.

I. A person. A person crawls as an infant ("the morning"), walks on two legs for most of their life ("noon"), and uses a cane to walk as they get older ("the evening"). This is known as the Riddle of the Sphinx, because it first appeared in a Greek play and was posed by a mythical creature called a sphinx.

J. A hole

K. One keeps the lawn wet and the other keeps the laun-dry.

L. TWOS-day

M. A kite

N. A stamp

O. The ace of hearts. In most decks, this card has a single large heart in the middle.

P. FRY-day

Q. A candle

R. Sunglasses

S. A piano

T. Dice

U. One is a tasteful whale and one is a wasteful tale.

V. A pillow

W. An anchor

X. Sand

Y. They sleep at night.

Z. A photograph

CLUES

Level 1: Smarty-pants

1. Try brainstorming possible answers based on the first part of the clue, "something you do while . . . your teacher is teaching." What are some things you can do while your teacher is teaching?

2. The Y in the last ditloid stands for "years."

3. Each step of this journey will last 1½ minutes: 1 minute of climbing, and 30 seconds of rest. How far does Shelley get during each step? Figuring this out will help you calculate how many minutes she needs. Remember, the last "rest" will be after she's reached the top and won't impact her time!

4. Try making a list of words that fit the description. What are some vehicles that can go fast?

5. Try thinking about each part of the puzzle individually. For example, first think about what a hen's baby is called. Next, think about a vegetable that comes from a pod.

6. If Bip were a liar, would they tell you they were a liar?

7. Try covering up the second word with your finger so that it doesn't distract you. What compound words can you make with the first word? Then uncover the second word and see if any of your ideas work with it as well. The second word link includes another name for a "lightning bug."

8. Since the four digits don't occur more than once and they only add up to 10, you can narrow down the possible options.

9. Reread the question and make sure you know what the puzzle is asking.

10. It can be useful to make a grid to help you solve this kind of logic puzzle. For each piece of information that you get in the text, put an X (no) or an O (yes) in the related box.

Example: "Jasmine baked the almond cookies right before the yogurt cake." Therefore, the almond cookies cannot be last.

	1	2	3
Meskouta			
Almond Cookies			X
Yogurt Cake			

11. You can use your fingers to cover up various sticks, which may help you visualize your options.

12. In this type of puzzle, it's important to notice details, like where the words are placed. The "secret" that's circled here is the one at the top. Can you think of any sayings that use that word?

13. A prime number is only divisible by 1 and itself. You can easily list all the prime numbers between 1 and 20 and use trial and error. You can also try working backward from 30 by reversing the operations. This means your first step would be to add 3 to 30.

14. It looks like the fourth word is "loud"!

15. You can start at the top or bottom, if you think you know one of those words. For the word after "SEAN," you'll change the last letter.

16. What characteristics does each object have? Sometimes it can be helpful to list things you know about the objects, such as what color they are or how each one tastes.

17. The third word refers to a bird losing its feathers.

18. It can help to break the puzzle apart into steps. Step one: Who is the brother of your father's only sister? Step two: Who is the child of that person?

19. If Yeison has six pennies, that's the least possible amount of money he has. You can substitute dimes one at a time to get all possible amounts.

20. This is a pattern. What is the next step?

Level 2: Prodigy

21. Use this grid to help you solve the puzzle. In the future, you can create these grids anytime you need to compare information. Put an X in any box that is not true and an O in any box that is true. Therefore, fact 1 (Jayna is 10 years old) gives you this information:

	8	9	10	March	August	October
Jayna	X	X	O			
Olivia			X			
Azeema			X			
March						
August						
October						

22. This spoonerism swaps the B sound.

23. You can work on anagrams by brainstorming possible answers for either word. It seems like the second word is easier.

24. To do this exercise, you'll need a bar or a doorframe—something you can grab above your head.

25. Since the hundreds column of the product is 4, you know that the multiplier cannot be greater than 4. You also can assume that it won't be 1, since no number is repeated and 1 multiplied by anything is itself. Start using trial and error with either 2 or 3 in the multiplier position.

26. The third item is a fairytale that involves a brick house.

27. Remember, this puzzle is easiest if you figure out how far Shelley can go in each step of the journey. Each step is made up of 1 minute of climbing and 30 seconds of rest.

28. The second word could complete the phrase "Look out _____!"

29. These statements contradict each other! One of them is lying, but who?

30. An "in-law" is someone who is related by marriage. So, for example, your brother-in-law would be the husband of your sibling.

31. You may need a mirror to figure it out!

32. If you need help visualizing, you can draw Kamu's card on a piece of paper.

33. This puzzle is about mice . . . three of them.

34. Do some brainstorming. What are all the words you can think of to describe each of the parts? Here's a hint: the breakfast food has many different names, depending on where you live.

35. This is a good opportunity for some trial and error. Each time you try numbers, you'll find out whether your answers are far too big or too small. For example, you'll quickly discover that $8{,}888 \times 8{,}888$ is waaay too large, but that $8{,}888 \div 8{,}888$ is only one. (Hint: The final number sentence uses only addition.)

36. When you're solving this type of puzzle, think of the objects from as many angles as possible. The answer may lie in a part of the object or its color. It may also have something to do with what you use the object for. In this instance, it's a part of each object.

37. Be sure to count squares of different sizes.

38. The thing that buckles is a belt.

39. Try doing this puzzle with toothpicks or cotton swabs to figure it out.

40. The words "before all else" tell you where to look for the hidden word. "Considerate" is a hint for what the hidden word is.

Level 3: Brainiac

41. Luckily, you don't need to figure out all the house colors of all the people—just the person living in the gray house.

42. Start by figuring out how many of each coin Dylan has.

43. The first word is a position in Quidditch, the sport from *Harry Potter*.

44. "GO" has to be big enough to create a three-digit number when doubled. Remember to rely on trial and error! Making mistakes brings you closer to the right answer.

45. It can help to draw this out. You can also try playing with sticky notes on the sides of a tissue box. Remember, if you have a cube, painting two sides with a shared edge can be flipped to look like other versions, no matter which two adjacent sides you paint.

46. Take a look at Simone's and Ingrid's statements. One of them is telling the truth.

47. The third word may be new to you, but it shares three of its letters with a farm animal. It means "to provoke or annoy."

48. Use this table to help you plan each raft trip. The first one has been done for you. Remember the rules of who eats what, if left alone! F = Farmer, W = Wolf, G = Goat, C = Cabbage

STARTING POINT	ON THE RAFT	FAR BANK
W + C	F + G →	

49. To solve this problem, consider what would happen if you drew a different-colored marble each time. How many would you have drawn before drawing your next one makes a matched pair?

50. The second part is a common pet.

51. Baseball; fun to ride; go fish!

52. Look for common words, like "and" and "the." This will help you solve the rest.

53. The best way to solve this is with trial and error. You'll quickly figure out if you need a higher or lower number of boxes.

54. What can you do *to* all of these things?

55. The hint "lastly" tells you where in the words to find the answer. "Animals" tells you what you're looking for.

56. You will land on the square next to START for your first move.

57. Pay special attention to the beginnings and ends of words.

58. The third step is a medieval weapon or a spray someone may use to defend themselves.

59. You can start with either clue. Do you know the name of the person who makes sure players are following the rules in baseball? If not, try the other clue: what do you call a large area under the control of one person? (Hint: It's not "kingdom," even though a king does control a kingdom. Can you think of other words like this?)

60. When you fold a section of paper, you create two new sections.

Level 4: Mastermind

61. Take a look at clues 1 and 2 together. Based on those clues, what do you know about the topping Mahé got? (Hint: There's only one possible option left!)

62. Like paired anagrams, you can brainstorm possible words for each hint. The easier part of the puzzle is the word for a "brilliant new contraption." What would you call one of these—particularly if it's brand-new to the world?

63. Remember, you compute the numbers in parentheses first.

64. In the first column, one of the letters is also a complete word. Which of the two letters is this true for? Put that in the bottom left box.

65. Because Sara says that Kofi is the knight, Sara cannot be a knight.

66. What words do you think of when you think of ice? Can you think of a rock band whose name has any of those words? The band is still active today!

67. Start by making 30 out of 7, 6, and 2.

68. Your squares do not have to be the same size. (Hint: There are five squares in the picture as given.)

69. Since Ace can't move diagonally, you must first move them right and then up.

70. Here, you're not looking for just one answer—you're considering possibilities.

71. The last item has to do with famous landmarks.

72. Same as before, look for common words, like "and" and "the." This will help you solve the rest.

73. The third word is a bluish-green color.

74. Since none of the bags are labeled correctly, that tells you a lot.

75. The second word is what you do with clothes.

76. Begin with the second part of the problem. What is the relationship between the three men in "that man's father is my father's son"?

77. Remember to think about the question in as many ways as possible. Do these things have anything in common in size, location, or color?

78. The middle number is 5.

79. How do you keep your gift amount secret from the next person when you pass the calculator?

80. Read the letters alone. What word is formed?

Level 5: Genius

81. To save time, have the two slowest people (C & D) cross the bridge together. You can have the fastest person available on the ending side return the torch to the start.

82. Try adding or subtracting numbers from each existing number to try to see a pattern. You'll find the answer in an equation that you can apply to each number.

83. The answer has something to do with how each of these items (planet, state, bird) compares to other items in their categories.

84. The first puzzle solution is one word. The second solution is three words. The first word in the second solution is "no." You may want to write the letters of the first solution down out of order so that your brain can imagine them in new ways.

85. You can set up this problem as an equation, starting with the third pet, which is the lightest:

$x + 3x$ (This is the weight of the third pet plus the second pet. Now we'll add in the first pet.)
$x + 3x + 6x$ (The first pet is twice as heavy as the second pet.)
$x + 3x + 6x = 20$
$10x = 20$

How much is x? When you plug this back into your original equation, you'll get each pet's weight.

86. Try using each word in a sentence.

87. Because the answer is a four-digit number, L must be 1 or 2 since nothing is carried over. You can play around with trial and error as you continue.

88. The first part of the clue is a large animal.

89. Without a preposition, this word is what you do with a baby.

90. Since queens attack in every direction, you'll need to make sure no two queens are in the same row ("rank" in chess terms), column ("file"), or diagonal path.

91. The second number will remain zero.

92. This rebus puzzle is a bit of a math joke. Do you know what the number 3.14159 is called?

93. There are only two people in this situation.

94. To get the highest possible product, you'll have to use the highest numbers (5 and 6) in the hundreds columns.

95. You know M must be 1 because no combination of four-digit numbers would require you to carry 2 (even 9,999 + 9,999 = 19,998, with a 1 in the ten thousands column).

96. "A fruit" is your indicator of what type of answer you're looking for.

97. This is a great opportunity for trial and error, since the total is only 30 years.

98. Your row of three won't move. You can also practice with real pennies!

99. Without a preposition, this is what monkeys do, or what you do on the monkey bars.

100. You might be thinking, *He can just turn it diagonal*, and you're right, but he can't take it on the bus that way. He'll need to find or purchase another item to help him out.

BRAIN TEASER ANSWERS

Level 1: Smarty-pants

1. listen/silent

2. 7 days in a week; 28 days in February; 10 years in a decade

3. 7 minutes. Shelley progresses 1½ feet every minute, so it will take her 4 minutes to climb 6 feet and then 1 minute to climb the final 4 feet. However, she has to take a total of four (30-second) breaks, meaning her total time is 7 minutes.

4. RACECAR

5. Chickpea

6. Bip is a liar and Bop is a truth-teller. Bip cannot be a truth-teller, because then they would tell you they were a truth-teller. Bip must be a liar since they are stating that both they and Bop are liars. Since Bip is lying, Bop can't be a liar. Therefore, Bop must be a truth-teller.

7. FAIRY (tooth fairy, fairy tale), FLY (firefly, fly ball), TAPE (masking tape, tape measure)

8. 4,132

9. 3. The question says, "all but 3 of them," meaning all the players except 3 were in the Taffy Shop, so 3 were left in the rain.

10. Meskouta (first), almond cookies (second), yogurt cake (third)

11.

12. Top secret

13. 11

14. READ THIS OUT LOUD: FLARKSPURIANS ARE SMARTER THAN WITLOOMITES. HAHA!

15. SEAL, SELL, SILL

16. Lemonade is a liquid; the rest of the objects are solid.

17. MOLE, MOLT, MOAT

18. It's you! If your father's sister only has one brother, your father must be that person. Since he is your father, and you are an only child, you must be the person mentioned in the puzzle.

19. 6¢, 15¢, 24¢, 33¢, 42¢, 51¢, 60¢

20. 10 (adds a row of 4), 15 (adds a row of 5), 21 (adds a row of 6), 28 (adds a row of 7), 36 (adds a row of 8)

Crystal Challenge #1 Answer: WATERFALL

Level 2: Prodigy

21. Jayna is 10 and was born in March; Olivia is 8 and was born in August; Azeema is 9 and was born in October.

22. A well-oiled bicycle

23. spark/parks

24. pull-up

25. $154 \times 3 = 462$

26. *101 Dalmatians*; *Snow White and the Seven Dwarfs*; "3 Little Pigs"

27. 4 minutes. In 1 minute of climbing and 30 seconds of rest, Shelley makes 2½ feet of progress up the hill. In 3 minutes (two cycles of walking and resting), she makes 5 feet of progress. In her final minute, she makes it the last 5 feet to the top.

28. elbow/below

29. Skeetle is telling the truth and Skootle is lying.

30. Your mother

31. "Every great dream begins with a dreamer."
—Harriet Tubman

32.

33. Three blind mice (because they are missing their eyes ["i"s])

34. Flapjack

35. 888 + 88 + 8 + 8 + 8 = 1,000

36. They all have keys.

37. 30: 16 (1×1) squares; 9 (2×2) squares; 4 (3×3) squares; 1 (4×4) square

38. BELL, BELT, BEAT

39.

40. Nice: **N**oona **is c**onsiderate **e**ver.

Crystal Challenge #2 Answer: JAR. All the other words spell another English word when written backward: pot (top), rat (tar), dog (god), and ton (not).

Level 3: Brainiac

41. Staci. She cannot live in the green house (clue 1), the blue house (clue 2), or the red house (clue 3).

42. $3.21. Dylan has 20 coins, so 10 coins ($\frac{1}{2}$) are quarters, or $2.50; 4 coins ($\frac{1}{5}$) are nickels, or $0.20; and 5 coins ($\frac{1}{4}$) are dimes, or $0.50. One penny is $0.01.

43. chaser/search

44. 50 + 50 = 100

45. 10 ways: 6 gold sides (1 total), 6 black sides (1 total), 1 gold and 5 black (1 total), 1 black and 5 gold (1 total), 3 black and 3 gold (2 total: three sides meeting at a corner, and three sides in a line), 2 gold and 4 black (2 total), 2 black and 4 gold (2 total)

46. Ingrid is the thief.

47. LOAD, GOAD

48. There are a few variations to this answer, but all agree that it takes multiple trips! Here's one possibility: Take the goat over. Return alone. Take the wolf over. Return with the goat. Take the cabbage over. Return alone. Take the goat over.

STARTING POINT	ON THE RAFT	FAR BANK	
F, W, G, C	–	–	
W + C	F + G →		Trip #1 ends with F + G on far bank
W + C	← F	G	Trip #2 ends with W, C, and F at start
W	F + C →	G	Trip #3 ends with F, G, and C on far bank
W	← F + G	C	Trip #4 ends with F, G, and W at start
G	F + W →	C	Trip #5 ends with F, W, and C on far bank
G	← F	W + C	Trips #6 and #7 retrieve G

49. 4. If you drew a black marble, a blue marble, and a purple marble, you'd have 3 marbles. Your next marble, number 4, is guaranteed to match one that you've already drawn.

50. Hotdog

51. 3 strikes and you're out; 2 wheels on a bicycle; 52 cards and 2 jokers in a deck of cards

52. (1) *Moana* (2016), (2) *Cars* (2006), (3) *The Princess and the Frog* (2009), (4) *Beauty and the Beast* (1991), (5) *How to Train Your Dragon* (2010), (6) *Finding Nemo* (2003), (7) *Home* (2015), (8) *Red Shoes and the Seven Dwarfs* (2019)

53. 11. The most obvious possible answer would be 10, which is 8 boxes of 10 small toys (80 toys) plus 2 boxes of 8 large toys (16 toys). However, this does not meet the requirement of Jacinta having more large pet toys than small ones. The answer is: 7 boxes of 8 large toys (56 toys) + 4 boxes of 10 small toys (40 toys).

54. You can carve them. Sometimes people carve their initials into things, like trees!

55. Dogs: Lastly, animals delighte**d to** wa**g** tail**s.**

56.

		🌀
		↑
START →	→	

57. (1) Lion: For rea**l, I on**ly want to play video games. (2) Camel: Don't pani**c! A mel**ting chocolate bar still tastes good. (3) Yak: Tala**ya k**icked the ball and scored a goal. (4) Anteater: **Can tea ter**rify you? Just ask Reuven.

58. MATS, MATE, MACE

59. umpire/empire

60. 32 sections

Crystal Challenge #3 Answer: RAINBOW

61. Gaspard: strawberry with cherries; Mahé: vanilla with caramel; Yuma: mint with peanuts; Anna: chocolate with fudge

62. intention/invention

63. $(\frac{2}{1}) + (3 \times 4) = 14$

64. "There are so many things I want to do, so many things I have to say."

65. Kofi is the knight. That means that Sara is telling the truth. Therefore, Sara is the spy (who can tell the truth or lie). Maritza is the knave.

66. Coldplay

67.

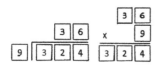

68.

69. →↑→→↑→

70. There are two possible answers to this puzzle. Tim could be either Cooper's father or his uncle. Given that Cooper's grandmother must have more than one child, Tim could be married to Cooper's mother and still have a sister-in-law. Tim could also be married to one of Cooper's mother's siblings and be Cooper's uncle.

71. 26 letters of the alphabet; 12 signs of the zodiac; 7 Wonders of the World

72. (1) *Percy Jackson and the Lightning Thief* (Rick Riordan), (2) *A Wrinkle in Time* (Madeleine L'Engle), (3) *A Long Walk to Water* (Linda Sue Park), (4) *Matilda* (Roald Dahl), (5) *El Deafo* (Cece Bell), (6) *Ghosts* (Raina Telgemeier), (7) *Out of My Mind* (Sharon Draper), (8) *Hurricane Child* (Kacen Callender)

73. HEAL, TEAL, TELL, TALL

74. One. You only need to draw one marble from the bag labeled "mixed." You know this bag contains either black marbles or white marbles because it cannot contain both. If you draw one black marble, you'll know that it's the black bag and that the bag labeled "white" is actually the mixed bag. If you draw one white marble, you'll know that it's the white bag and that the bag labeled "black" is actually the mixed bag.

75. WEAR, HEAR, HEAD, HERD, HERE, HIRE, FIRE

76. The person in the photograph is the speaker's son.

77. They are all yellow.

78.

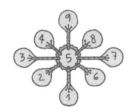

These numbers can shift around, as long as the three numbers in each line stay together.

79. Enter a fake amount of money into the calculator before passing it. Don't forget this number! Each of your friends adds their amounts before passing it to the next person. When it gets back to you, subtract the fake amount of money. Now add the real amount of money you received and divide the total by five. You'll have your answer!

80. Safety in numbers

Crystal Challenge #4 Answer: CRYSTAL

_T_ 1. YUCK/TUCK
_R_ 2. ROPE
_L_ 3. HOP/HOOP/LOOP
_Y_ 4. FOREVER – FOR (FOUR) = EVER(Y)
_C_ 5. ONE + C = CONE
_A_ 6. LONE + A = ALONE
_S_ 7. TON/TONE/STONE

Level 5: Genius

81. A, B, C, and D are on the starting side. A and B cross at B's speed—4 minutes. A returns the torch in 2 minutes, so now 6 minutes have elapsed. Next, C and D cross at D's speed—16 minutes. When they arrive, 22 total minutes have elapsed. B is waiting for them and returns the torch to the starting side in 4 minutes. When B arrives, 26 total minutes have elapsed. A and B cross together at B's speed—4 minutes. When they arrive, everyone is together and 30 minutes have elapsed.

82. 127. Each jump between numbers is 2N + 1. 2(3) + 1 = 7, 2(7) + 1 = 15, . . .

83. They are the largest of their kind.

84. astronomers/no more stars

85. First pet: 12 pounds; second pet: 6 pounds; third pet: 2 pounds

86. Marker. The other words have two pronunciations, depending on whether they are a noun or a verb. Read these two sentences out loud: "Luke fought with the rebels to bring down the Empire." "Leia wanted to rebel against Darth Vader." In the first sentence, the emphasis is on the first syllable and "bel" sounds like "bull." In the second sentence, the emphasis is on the second syllable and it sounds like "bell." Try this with the other words!

87. L = 2, M = 1, N = 7, and O = 8

88. Horseradish

89. Hold. Hold up (meaning "to delay") and hold on (meaning "to grip").

90. The mirror image of this is also correct.

91.

92. Piece of pie(π)

93. They are standing back-to-back.

94. $641 \times 532 = 341,012$

95. $9,567 + 1,085 = 10,652$

96. Grape: Un**p**redictably, a fruit g**r**owing cluster**e**d **at** ha**p**py vin**e**yards.

97. Mr. Mittens is 15, Irving is 10, and Peppa is 5.

98. Here is one possibility. There are 12 total solutions, and all of them involve similar spacing and configurations.

99. Hang. Hang on (meaning "wait up!") and hang out (meaning "to spend time together").

100. Keshun needs to find a box to put the walking stick in that is 4 feet long and at least 3 feet wide. Then he can place the stick in the box diagonally and safely take it on the bus.

Crystal Challenge #5 Answer:

1. Vermont 2. Texas 3. Iowa 4. Nevada 5. Oregon 6. Oklahoma 7. Arizona 8. Utah 9. Missouri 10. New Jersey 11. Georgia 12. Nebraska 13. Kentucky 14. California 15. Illinois 16. Ohio 17. Arkansas 18. Rhode Island 19. Idaho 20. Alaska 21. Michigan 22. New Hampshire 23. Maine 24. Wyoming 25. Wisconsin
Secret word: FLORIDA

FINAL CRYSTAL CHALLENGE ANSWER

A B C D E F G H I

J K L M N O P Q R

S T U V W X Y Z

WE NEVER THOUGHT

WITLOOMITES

WOULD SOLVE OUR

TRICKY PUZZLES!

THE CRYSTAL IS

HIDDEN IN A

GREEN JAR AT

RAINBOW SPRINGS

WATERFALL IN

FLORIDA.

FURTHER READING

Has all this puzzle-solving made you hungry for more brain teasers? Here are some books and websites that might interest you. It's good to practice in case Ace needs your help in the future!

Math Riddles for Smart Kids by M. Prefontaine

One-Minute Mysteries and Brain Teasers by Sandy Silverthorne and John Warner

The 125 Best Brain Teasers of All Time by Marcel Danesi, PhD

The Brainiest Insaniest Ultimate Puzzle Book! by Robert Leighton, Mike Shenk, and Amy Goldstein

The Challenging Riddle Book for Kids by Danielle Hall

Tough Riddles for Smart Kids by Jenny Moore

Kids.NIEHS.NIH.gov/games/brainteasers/index.htm: This page, on the National Institute of Environmental Health Sciences website, is full of number games, riddles, rebuses, and more for kids to enjoy.

Puzzlemaker.DiscoveryEducation.com: Do you feel like trying your hand at creating some teaser puzzles? This site from Discovery Education lets you make cryptograms, math teasers, hidden messages, and more!

Brainzilla.com: For kids who want more challenging puzzles, Brainzilla has a great mix of games to develop your skills. Logic problems, word puzzles, and fun games like dominoes and sudoku are available.

ABOUT THE AUTHOR

 **Danielle Hall** has loved puzzles from an early age and enjoyed old computer games like *The 7th Guest* and *Myst*. She has 10 years of teaching experience, including in North Carolina, Puerto Rico, and Germany. Currently, she makes digital escape games for middle and high schoolers. Danielle loves reading, running, and swing dancing. One day, she hopes to visit Machu Picchu. She lives with her wife and pets Padfoot and Crookshanks in Astoria, Oregon. Visit her at TeachNouvelle.com.

CPSIA information can be obtained
at www.ICGtesting.com
Printed in the USA
JSHW021003040621
15324JS00004B/5